Special Characters

Copyright © 2024 Sam Powney

Published by Trivial Disaster Publishing

All rights reserved.

Cover art by Roderick Brydon (KLR Covers)

ISBN: 9798872100331

Sam Powney

TRIVIAL DISASTER PUBLISHING

Contents

Old News 1

    Plantlife 2
    A Shropshire verse 3
    Deplorable 6
    Brexit 7
    Megxit 8
    Russia's problem 9
    Festering 11
    Limericks 11
    AUKUS 11
    Titanic 11

Surreal Truths 13

    Table with eight legs 14
    Modernity 15
    Cat 16
    Escape 18
    Business email 19
    The ballad of the stone 20
    Journey of a thousand miles 24
    Salvage 26

My Dahk Lady 27

    Sorry 28
    Middle management 28
    Vroom vroom pantoum 29
    Security 30

 Tunnel boring 31
 Bridge 33
 Food & Environmental Hygiene Department report 35
 Begpackers 38
 Immigration Tower 39

Personas 41
 A clownfish responds 42
 Gainful employment 45
 Victims 46
 Bat-slapped 48
 My future trial 50
 Needs 52
 The craft 53
 A whisky bottle speaks 54
 Blasphemy 56
 Contemporary cupid 57
 Expeliamus 58

Beliefs and opinions 61
 Election pitch 62
 Anthem 63
 Heaven 64
 Evopsych 65
 Enlightenment 67
 Internet discussion 69
 Breakthrough innovation 70
 Manuela 71

Written word 73
   To En (–) 74
   Writer's block 75
   Centre-justified 76
   Slippery Sam 77
   Shake n bake 79
   Auto-Shakespeare 80
   Bottom line 81
   Translation 1 82
   Returning from Baidi town at dawn 84
   Translation 2 85

Attempts at non-humour 87
   Cynicism 88
   Brancusi's Bird in Space 91
   Great and small 92
   Memories of Margaret 93
   Uses for a flag 94
   The project 95
   Addicts 96
   Mujo 99
   Great resignation 100

Acknowledgements 103

For Yiran

Old News

Plantlife

(Advice for listeners of the BBC's *Gardener's Question Time*, c. 2006)

Your rose is withered and forlorn;
can nothing save its blackened thorn?
I recommend a cure that will:
Selected works of Kim Jong Il!
A reading every noon and night
will radically change its plight,
and where before the petals fell
new buds will soon begin to swell.

Iranian uranium
is best for your geranium.
And if it's still a little sad,
a speech of Ahmedinejad,
transmitted live from Isfahan
on Press TV or Voice of Iran,
is guaranteed to bring it round
and make a difference most profound.
But for an even healthier glow,
try "Hezbollah's Magic Multigrow".

Resist the gardener's common urge
to fault each autocratic purge
in countries whose political slants
will likely cheer your garden plants.
For nature is, beneath the sun,
at root totalitarian.
To those who loathe the scorpions' whip
and criticize dictatorship
in Pyongyang, Yangon, or Khartoum,
I say…let a hundred flowers bloom!

A Shropshire verse

(Nov 2016)

Lord Barry is a noble man.
He's always done the best he can
to keep the manor house protected.
And yet, this week, he is ejected!
His bills have all come due at last
and we poor peasants are aghast
to see our master dispossessed –
the fall of an heraldic crest.

And what new money takes his place?
A most ignoble orange face.
This upstart lacks the courteous graces
that marked our former lord and ladies.
He threatens us with swift dismissal
and posts derogatory epistles
on yonder church-door; very short
they are, and written just for sport.
He's shouted oaths at groundsman Craig
and made a pass at all the milkmaids.
He says he'll burn the fields and barns,
chop down the woods and sell the farms.
He's vowed to work us morn till eve
building walls to keep out thieves.

Each soul runs scared in Manor House
from man, to horse, to scullery mouse.
So Barry gathers all together,
to reassure us in the foyer.

"Dear manor folk, of whom I'm one,
Fear not the future, carry on!
This house is built on firm foundations –
that's you, no matter what your station,

who in your daily toil and service
give succour to the greater purpose.
I know your loyalty to this place
will drive you at the faster pace
demanded by the orange man.
He has a rather different plan
from mine on how to run the show.
Nil desperandum, tally ho!
You should be proud to be a part
of Manor House with all your heart.
Besides, he has my signature
that you come with the furniture.
Farewell, we must away down south
to our Dordogne summer house."

Now, hearing Barry thus extol
the virtue of our manor roles
and urge compliance on us all
as part of some imagined whole,
I see him in a different light
and question if I've had him right.
I start to reassess my faith in
Barry's genuine motivations.
I'm wondering if this enterprise
is built on lots of pretty lies
that take advantage of our need
to feel a group identity.
And maybe I should leave for town
before the manor house falls down.

Deplorable

(31 Oct 2020)

Look, I could talk about BLM and Antifa,
and George Soros and the globalist agenda,
and Mexican-Chinese-gender-neutral toilets.
And sure, I can even roll off
Jordan Peterson's 12 rules for life.
But I don't really care about gun rights.
I'm not angry about safe zones
or affirmative action or postal votes.
Mainly, I just liked *The Apprentice*.
so I like *him*, a genuine celebrity.

Not like Joe Biden – never seen him on anything.
He's a nobody. Never been entertained by him.
He won't even get in a slinging match…
now I ask you, where's the fun in that?
What's the point in running for president
if you're not going to get down and scrap for it?

But my man's a bona fide somebody –
a known, certifiable entity.
And yes, maybe he paid for that magic,
but the important thing is that he's got it.
I buy the brand, I follow the man.
Big man, right man, my man.
Big tie, big suit, big house, big job.
Make the big bigger.
Make the biggest big that's ever been bigged!
MAGA!!!

Brexit

(2016)

To be sure, your island is sacred,
your identity's precious as gold.
You need to make sure it's protected
and preserved from the rest of the world.

For your ways and traditions are noble
and your history shines like a star.
Your democracy's second to none
and is envied by those near and far.

Your parliament's strong and efficient
and its members are honest and true.
Your political parties care firstly
for the general good, win or lose.

Your food is the finest in Europe,
and your weather is endlessly fair.
Your trains are always on time
and your prince has a full head of hair.

You've planned in advance for the future
by investing in promising fields
and prepared for the threat of computers
making millions of jobs obsolete.

So hurrah for the coming of freedom
again to its rightful abode,
a resounding proof in our era
that a nation can go it alone.

Megxit

(Jan 2020)

You will no doubt have heard the news
that sets our lives and hopes askew.
No, not the missiled airplane, nor
the death that nearly sparked a war.
And not the apocalyptic flames
that sweep the antipodean plane.
These events, though tragic ones,
but pale in comparison
to tidings that a royal prince
and princess have announced they'll rinse
their hands of all responsibility
and distance themselves from public duty.
With this, the ungracious pair aspire
to escape the tabloids and retire
across the Atlantic, as if they're owed
the right to live as separate souls.
They even lacked the grace to wait
for granny to approve their flight.
For what else is this rash retreat
than <u>abdication</u> from our needs?
I ache to think of the tasks unfilled
now they've given up royal roles:
parades un-viewed by princely eyeballs,
chests bereft of glittering medals;
the ribbons uncut, hands unshaken…
a great dearth of awkward conversations.
Such horrors and more this move portends.
We live in dark days indeed, my friends.

Russia's problem

(Feb 2023)

The Kremlin's conundrum
is undoubtedly tough.
We all see the problem:
Russia's not big enough.

Russia's not big enough –
everyone says it.
In Russia, they're stuffed
like coats in a closet.

Everyone says it,
they're packed like sardines.
Russia needs an exit
or it simply can't breathe.

They're packed like sardines
from Yakutsk to Murmansk.
In the space in between,
you can't swing a cat.

From Yakutsk to Murmansk,
it's wall-to-wall Russians;
Siberia's a shark tank
and the Arctic is busting.

It's wall-to-wall people,
not like here in Hong Kong,
where we all live like eagles –
wings outstretched and alone.

Not like us in Hong Kong,
Russia's number one challenge
is the numberless throng
filling each street and passage.

Russia's number one challenge
as Putin understands,
yes, its only thing lacking,
is the need for more land.

Festering

(Nov 2023)

We used to pin the dead
to their coffins
with a stake through the heart.
But now I hear
that David Cameron
has been raised to the Lords
and will soon be abroad,
shuttling across the skies.
Such are the end times.

Limericks

AUKUS

(Sep 2021)

There is no greater blow to one's ego
than a submarine deal torpedoed.
"Cher Scottie, non!"
cries the stranded Macron
to a periscope out in the billows.

Titanic

I watched from a rowboat that night
and wept for the many who died.
But more troubling by far
was the state of my car
after young Jack and Rose got inside.

Surreal Truths

Table with eight legs

Surreal times one – André Breton
Ism times two – Manifeste du
Ivre stage three – Yves Tanguy
Fire times four – Spain's at war
Canvas times five – Guggenheim buys
Dollars times six – Dali is a fascist
Books times seven – coffee-table Taschen
Fridge magnets x8 and a T-shirt Magritte

Modernity

English is too globalized,
I decided.
So I made an indelible mark
in the most esoteric script
known to man,
but not unknown
to my tattoo artist.
Three ancient symbols, she said,
distil deep poetic meaning:
"Wisdom grows like bamboo:
slow at first, then fast as a dragon."
It defines my bicep
and my truth:
现
代
性

Cat

Let's put it this way:
you like sitting.
If possible, you sleep most of the day.
But when the doorbell rings, you hide,
scuttling into the darkest corner.

Games obsess you,
you can't help yourself chasing after baubles.
You cackle for hours
at the flickering light on the wall
in the long afternoon.

You don't drink enough water.
You're fussy about food,
but guzzle every morsel of your favourites,
and the smell of treats
send you into a frenzy.
You're getting a bit on the heavy side.

I'd tell you to change your lifestyle,
but what do I know.
I'm just your cat.

Escape

(2009)

We leave these boxes of the mind,
your circles and your triangles.
Your matrices and graphs we find
as bankrupt as financials.

Your spreadsheet mesh is shutting down,
your currencies are paper thin,
your border lines are pointless now,
your edifice is sinking.

Your sharp lapels are fading fast –
the earth shook out your gridlines.
Regard your buildings washing past,
your pylons skittled wide.

Your chessboard mind recedes from view,
your cubicles corrupted.
Your margins slipped away from you,
your lines of thought disrupted.

The sunlight's warped your frame of mind
the stucco's rent with wrinkles.
Your cornerstones and paradigms
are crumbling into shingle.

Your numbers fail to match the count,
you've lost the beat, your rhythm's late.
The infinite has looped you round
and tightens like a rat snake.

We leave you in your office blocks,
we're off to see the trees.
Goodbye to your atomic clocks
and death to all geometry!

Business email

Dear Valued Forward Slash,

I write with reference to your letter in reference to the reference letter as referred to me by the referred-to referee.

Firstly (though notwithstanding and without prejudice to the above), please accept our heartfelt gratitude for your gracious platitudes.

May I take this moment to opportune you with a fortunate sports sponsorship annuity opportunity. Please be assured that we take all measures to ensure your insurance is secure in all instances.

Further to and following the above, please kindly consider the generic jargon bullet points below:

- Streamline
- Black swan
- In the pipeline
- Processing
- Feedback
- Delicious

Kindly also be reminded to sign the reply slip as required by and in compliance with the Wine and Fine-dining Society terms & conditions and submit in triplicate as stipulated herein.

In the meantime, may I wish robust growth to you and your upstanding firm in the Year of the Cock.

Yours warmly formal,

Clippy

NB: In case of any discrepancy between the Chinese and English versions of this document, the discrepancy shall apply and prevail.

Greenwash: Before you think, just do it!

The ballad of the stone

Upon a mountain trail I stopped
to rest upon a handsome rock.
"Old stone," I said, "how many a year,
have you lain in this biosphere?
How many epochs in this place
have passed before your granite face
as ceaseless scenes upon a stage
since, what, the late Triassic age?
Or are you from the Paleozoic?
Forgive my ignorance, old stoic.
but what a miracle that man
can measure that entire span
since born amongst volcanic tuff
you took the igneous form…"

"Enough!"
a voice exclaimed. I started back
and clenched as with a heart attack.
At length I quavered, "Who was that?"

"Tis I, old stoic, you pompous prat,"
the voice went on, with deep derision
though nothing moved before my vision.
"My spirit can no longer brook
its scorn of rantings so mistook.
By all means hold your theories
of little men, if you so please.
But I resent your weaving me
into such base chronology.
To hear my person thus included
in human nonsense so deluded –
it really grates against my grain
and causes me peculiar pain
(as when one of my smaller kin

gets lodged inside your moccasin).
How arrogantly you suppose
that time like Zeno's river flows.
There's no such change from my perspective,"
he curtly ended his invective.

I scarcely knew which greater shock
to reel from – that this sapient rock
could speak my language, or his views,
which all my learning so abused.

"Wise boulder," I at length replied,
"forgive my scientific pride,
but surely you do not dispute
my species' knowledge absolute
of progress and of time's elapse…"

"It may strike you that way perhaps,"
the stone cut in, "but I don't see
such signs of temporality.
You living creatures pass me by:
you're born, you blossom, wither, die…
it's all the same from fall to summer,
one aeon's much alike another."

"I see," I said, and quickly hastened
to be polite, though sorely chastened.
"And by what name shall I address
The vessel of such rare sagesse?"

"Call me Peter if you want,"
he spoke in tone most nonchalant.

"Well, Peter, I'm most curious
How t'is you speak our language thus."

"We stones are very quick with tongues,"
he said, "and there are many among
your kind who pass this way each year.

Some talk, some leave their markings here.
Yes, oftentimes when nature calls
the issue on poor Peter falls.
And one young man…shall I be frank?
no, stay, there is no need to yank
yourself away like one possessed.
These scenes, at least as you'd profess,
passed in a bygone century
or in the future, as may be.
And time has washed all stain away –
if you believe in yesterdays."

I recomposed myself with haste
and conquered my pronounced distaste:
"Yet, in your state so solitary
you practice our vocabulary.
For with whom else can you converse?
Our absence must weigh as a curse."

"Not in the least!" the stone retorted,
"You've got the universe distorted
by thinking man preeminent
among your fellow habitants.
The wagtail's poetry is wasted
upon an ego so inflated.
The harmony of millipedes
is finer than your symphonies,
But you could never understand
expressions of a scale so grand.
As for the intercourse I share
with fellow rocks and streams and air,
the content's simply too profound
to translate into human sound,
though there are some of your kind who
have fathomed it, and will, and do.

"Well, Pete, if I may call you that,"

I answered, "It was nice to chat.
"You've humbled me and all my race,
but though you claim a timeless space,
yet I'll bestow a souvenir,
of such a nature 'twould appear,
was never yet by human left
upon your noble lithic heft.

So saying I scanned the scenery
and seeing nought but greenery,
I hoisted down my cotton slacks
and squatted where before I sat
to make a solid demonstration
of Newton's precepts and causation.

"What, Pete, no further oratory
to greet my proof posteriori?
Though I confess you're better suited
to stay in stony silence muted."

This said, I bid dear Pete goodbye
and started off most satisfied,
though vowing ne'er to speak my mind
again to ought but humankind.

Journey of a thousand miles

Tips for success in the world's most exciting emerging market

1. Work hard and play hard.
2. Impress people with your competence and passion for the work you do.
3. Find a mentor in a position of great authority.
4. Become indispensable to the everyday running of your organization or entity.
5. Win over the regional managers.
6. Take on a key advisory role to your boss's successor.
7. Initiate a bold campaign in the region of Luoyang.
8. Don't be afraid to be unpopular if you're getting results. You can't make an omelette without breaking a few legs.
9. Wait until your boss is on the way out, then accumulate direct control over all the key levers of power.
10. When he's gone, force the young successor to offer you total command.
11. Magnanimously refuse while accepting a major promotion.
12. Repeat the previous step several times before accepting the top job with great reluctance.
13. Wait a few months to have the young successor quietly disposed of.
14. Reward your allies with key posts and A) build a large monument or B) throw a banquet.
15. Have yourself named Emperor Wu.
16. Build unity by sending a large invasion force across the Yellow River.
17. Strategically, you need to control the region of Luoyang. Lay siege to the city.
18. Capture Luoyang and enslave its inhabitants.
19. Secure your northern frontier by marrying off your daughter to the Khan of the steppe barbarians. Enjoy the rugged landscapes, sweetie!

20. Failure is natural; it's important to accept setbacks and build on them.
21. Yes, that's right, you've lost control of Luoyang. It's almost as if the inhabitants didn't like you.
22. Massacre the population of Luoyang.
23. Take to drinking large amounts of alcohol and making impetuous decisions.
24. Dabble in religion.
25. Engage in "immoral games" with your palace eunuchs.
26. In a fit of paranoia, execute several of your close relatives.
27. Isn't it about time you thought about Luoyang again? Magnanimously spare the remaining population! You're welcome, people of Luoyang!
28. Health problems are unavoidable, which is why you need to find the elixir of immortality. It's definitely out there, you just have to find it.
29. Just in case...it's important you name your successor, but not too early, obviously. Best of all would be one of your younger sons with a long life ahead of them.
30. Of course, your successor will need someone to guide them through the first few years, but you have someone capable in mind: a strong right-hand man who's been dealing very effectively with the troubling new situation in Luoyang.

Salvage

Man.
Can he be saved?
Can some remnant,
broken and barnacled,
be heaved from the depths?

Is man a condemned construct?
Or can those rough, swollen timbers
be refashioned into a new coherence?

Has the clock run out on jock?
Or will a new masculine,
christened with fallibility,
groan stern-backwards down the slipway.

Are they gone:
the stallions
the supermen
the sigma, *stehpinkler* Siegfrieds?
Just a faded, mouldering
concept of the past.
Like polo shirts.

Or will we
one day
see a fresh breed
of waistcoat and hairy testicles
hoofing its path down D'Aguillar Street?

My Dahk Lady

Sorry

I wish that I could do what's right.
Unfortunately, my hands are tied.
Not literally, you know what I mean,
but by the powers behind the scenes.
Oh no, I'm technically in charge
and technically can give commands,
and actually can, but actually can't…
it's complicated, you understand.

Again, I'm sorry for the balls
I've made of things. It's not my fault –
I've very little room to function,
except for my powers as already mentioned.
I wish I didn't have to stay
and keep on messing up this way.
But now I'm not allowed to quit
even though nobody's actually said that.
Things will get better, not to worry,
and like I said, I'm really sorry.

Middle management

If you're unhappy, the boss is to blame.
If the boss is unhappy, you're in the frame!
I sit in the middle expressing concern
and strum on my fiddle while everything burns.

Vroom vroom pantoum

We need to bring back harmony,
order needs to be restored.
And this can only be achieved
using the long arm of the law.

For calm and order to be restored,
the surest method and the best
is sticking the long arm of the law
directly into a hornets' nest.

The surest method and the best
is reaching deep into that hole
in the middle of the hornets' nest.
Let's stretch that arm as far as it goes.

Can your hear from within the hole
that loud and rising high-pitched hum?
Now, stir your arm as fast as it goes.
with vigour now: vroom, vroom, vroom!

You see?
That rising swarm with its fevered hum
heralds a newfound harmony.
With a vigorous stir and a vroom, vroom, vroom
contented calm has been achieved.

Security

Isn't it nice to feel secure.
Nice to get back to normal,
nice and safe and normal.
Back to buying nice things
in the shopping malls
and sucking on a milky frappé,
licking the froth off your lips:
mmm, nnnmm, nnnmm,
mmm, nnnmm, nnmmm.
Then let the metro sway you
ever so gently
to and fro,
to and fro,
until you start to feel safe and sleepy.
Sleepy times...
Say goodnight to the nice policemen
on the platform.
Say thank you to Mummy LamLam.
Time to go back now,
back to how things used to be,
Sshhhh, sshhhh, sshhhh,
just like nothing happened.
Go to sleep now, everybody.
Sleepy-byes...

Tunnel boring

Our MTR stations
are efficient and clean,
but we can't furnish setting
to brighten the scene.

Moscow has Kievskaya,
Paris has Louvre,
London has Westminster,
Shanghai has Bund.

New York has Grand Central,
while Stockholm's lines
boast staggering ceilings
of unique design.

And Tashkent has breathtaking
stations galore.
But Hong Kong, sad to say it,
is a city too poor

to pay architects dues
for a station of style,
and instead we must make do
with monochrome tiles.

Hong Kong has no shows
of conspicuous wealth,
extravagant clothes,
or parades of the self.

We live close to nature
in a simple existence
and aspire to little
but the barest subsistence.

There are no wealthy people
among us to finance
a space to be proud of
or which can unite us.

A work so splendiferous
none can afford,
least of all penniless
MTR Corp.

We turn our backs on all
rank ostentation
as we trudge through banal,
unoriginal stations.

Bridge

What is this project?
How to describe it?
What is that lingering phrase on the tip of your tongue
that resists being spoken?
Ah, it is gone again,
escaped into the forest of uncertainty
with a crashing of branches.

A beast this large is more than mere steel and cement.
It lives and breathes mightily,
its flanks as dazzling as snow in the sunlight.

An architect notes that its pillars are sturdy,
like thick legs shimmering in the waves.

An engineer admires its curving suspension towers,
each narrowing to a fine point.
He proclaims it a work of great value.

A surveyor praises its tensile strength.
Like a long, flexible limb, it stretches out over the sea,
trumpeting a new dawn.

A cartographer measures the two stretches, gleaming
like the twin spans of a colossal brow that never forgets.

An accountant weighs up the costs,
and finds it to be a project of great bulk,
crunching through public funds with tremendous appetite.

A marketing consultant evaluates its public communications.
This, she feels, trails behind,
like a thin, bedraggled afterthought.

And we poets,
how do we celebrate this behemoth of bleached concrete,

this milky mammoth?
Will we be caught flat-footed?
No! We reveal its hidden achievement:
bridging that vast gulf between
government,
the construction industry,
and investment consortiums.

But a term to do it justice?
Perhaps that will always sit with us,
unconscious and unspoken,
like a huge blank shape concealed in our living room.

Food & Environmental Hygiene Department report

(Jul 2018)

On the surface of the case, we noted six relevant matters:

1. That an elderly woman was dragging a trolley full of waste cardboard on the street.
2. That she gave a piece of cardboard to a domestic helper who asked for it.
3. That she accepted one Hong Kong dollar given to her by the domestic helper.
4. That this constitutes an exchange and, as such, is an offence under the Public Hygiene and Municipal Services Ordinance.
5. That we are bound to uphold the Public Hygiene and Municipal Services Ordinance in all cases.
6. That it was therefore our duty to apprehend the woman in question.

Having apprehended her, we noted six further aspects to the case:

1. That she was 75 years old with health problems.
2. That while she pleaded with us to let her go, she did not contest the facts of the case.
3. That she had 34 dollars on her person.
4. That the reduced public transport fare for elderly passengers is two dollars.
5. That she would need enough money to cover the transport fare home, and the same amount to travel to the Western Magistrates Court for her court appearance in one week's time.
6. That she could therefore be released on bail for the neat and tidy sum of 30 dollars.

In response to the unwarranted media outcry relating to the case, we noted six further facets of the matter:

1. That we enforce the Public Hygiene and Municipal Services Ordinance to the letter and do not deviate from our guidelines.
2. That the law means nothing without enforcement. It cannot be bent without weakening its overall structure.
3. That it is for the courts to decide, and if necessary amend, the shape of the law, and not the job of the Food and Environmental Hygiene Department.
4. That this is how society functions in a clean, efficient, and hygienic manner.
5. That the matter in question should have been an open and shut case.
6. Notwithstanding the above, that it left a dry taste in the mouth.

Following uninvited attention from certain deviant elements in society, we noted six further sides to the case:

1. That they implied we cared more about our departmental deliverables than an elderly woman with health problems and low income.
2. That they portrayed our procedures as being rigid, conformist, and "square".
3. That they implied we were hollow vessels, empty of basic human empathy and common sense.
4. That they accused us of mindlessly adopting the cuboid nature of the city which surrounds us, or some such loose thinking.
5. That they drew a surreal connection between our orderly thought process and the essence of a cardboard box.
6. That your parcel has arrived, Madam…I mean…what were we saying?

Begpackers

Friends, nothing truly gets my goat
like impecunious western folk
who fund the luxury of travel
by busking change from passing locals.

I say this as a man who's known
no privilege, and as all I own
is solely down to my hard effort,
relying on no help whatsoever,
and as one who's dedicated
all my time to eradicating
injustice and inequality
across the breadth of this great city.

In fact, so successful have I been,
that now the most outrageous thing
in all Hong Kong that yet besets us
is slightly less deserving beggars.

And this is why I feel compelled
to post about it to the world.
For how could anyone better use
their talents than to air their views
on bums from wealthy lands like Spain
Moldova, Chile, and Ukraine?

Well, possibly, one higher goal
would be a pen a rhyming ode
picking a sardonic quarrel
with those outraged by petty problems.

Immigration Tower

Walk the frenetic causeway
over Wan Chai's bustling streets.
Cross Gloucester and Hennessy
to the tower of delice.

Eight floors of elegance,
escalators of soft style.
A sanctum of delicate
expressions and smiles.

Crinkle of a flotilla
of creased photocopies.
Aroma of fresh passport photos
and sensual humanity.

Stares and whispers
murmured and transient,
queues of coiffed hipsters –
definition of ambience!

Behind shaded counters
Immigration Department nymphs and fauns
gamble with infectious laughter
while deftly juggling forms.

An experience like heaven.
And I, a celestial being
at five foot seven,
can almost touch the ceiling.

Oh, to be seen,
Oh, to be there,
drinking it in –
pure Baudelaire!

Personas

A clownfish responds

(The Dec 2017 issue of *Coral Reefs* journal, published by the University of Wollongong and Southern Cross University, made global headlines with a study that found clownfish do not have individual personalities: "*Amphiprion latezonatus* showed no discernible individual personality traits but appeared to act as a group.")

A clownfish without a personality: Ha ha ha.
The jester of marine creatures with literally no sense of humour.
It's so ironic!

I survive on zooplankton; what were you expecting? Jacob Burckhardt's renaissance man?
Ellen de-fucking Generes?

And what about you? Ooh, a behavioural scientist carrying out obscure research on yet another species...how very original.

Oh no, please. Feel free to swim into my water column and evaluate my lack of individuality.
I'm sure that'll make for hilarious reading in your academic journal. I hope it ensures your funding for some more essential scientific research.

And thoroughly peer-reviewed too – that must have been comforting to an independent soul like yourself. What an achievement.

No, no. Now you deserve to relax. Put your feet up and enjoy your Netflix series, or was it a Marvel movie? Bet you like to listen to the Beatles every now and again. Partial to a bit of fusion cuisine perhaps? What a unique specimen you are!

Well, I'd better be on my way. Got to practice my circus routine. You know, with the pies and the unicycle. Oh no, that's right, I'm just a stripy fish with eel-related anxiety issues.

Oh one more thing: did you know that my fecal matter provides essential nutrients to the sea anemone and thus ensures the continuation of my ecosystem? But of course you do – after all, you've studied my habits exhaustively for the past 3 years. So you'll be aware that another thing we clownfish entirely lack is an appreciation of metaphor.

Gainful employment

I want more a meaningful job
he confided in a life coach.
Do you blog? said she.
I can jog, said he.
Take a hike, said she.
If you like, said he.
And that's how he became a penguinologist.

Victims

(Dedicated to Henrik Hoeg)

My country has a reputation
for planetary domination.
In times gone by the globe was pink –
my countrymen would rarely shrink
from meddling in far-off affairs
or wresting power no matter where.
(One of many similar seizures,
they had the cheek to call Rhodesia.)
We subjugated alien peoples
and propagated countless evils –
famines, massacres, and wars
and "expeditions" to distant shores,
inventing concentration camps
and arbitrary lines on maps,
deliberately exacerbating
pre-existing social tensions –
all carried off with confidence
and condescending haughtiness.

It comes as no surprise of course
that all such actions have a source;
for British actions east and west
arose from *post-traumatic stress* –
the memory of swords and shields...
a national wound that never healed.
We rarely openly confess
our wellspring of unhappiness,
yet every English breast is plagued
with nightmares from an earlier age –
of red-striped sails and dragon prows
and helmets with encrusted brows,
of monasteries' treasures pillaged

and many a defenceless village.
How many nights I've lain awake
attempting to forget the ache
of peasants mercilessly slain,
victims of a Viking raid.
It's hard to overcome, suppress
the impact of a pain so fresh...

I offer empire no pretence
of a supposed beneficence;
but if you seek to lay the blame,
look no further than the Danes.

Bat-slapped

(Mid-2020)

Now we have
dry claws for hands,
crouching in our burrows
with big, trembling eyes
and hoarded edibles,
dreading a lungful
of pangolin scales.

Three months ago, I wore a suit
and talked
at some length
about branding strategy.

My future trial

Ladies and gentlem…I mean to say fellow creatures of the jury, allow me this opportunity to plead my case before you.

Trying me retroactively for these "crimes" is, I have to say, deeply unjust. You must understand, things were very different in those days.

To take the first charge against me: I cannot adequately defend myself for my part in climate change, except to say that I was a product of my age. I tried to consume as little as possible, and have earnestly revered Global Secretary Thunberg from the first time I heard her name. May the windmills be my witness.

On the second count, I unequivocally protest my innocence. At no time was I ever involved in, nor did I ever condone, the trading of cryptocurrency. True, I did not oppose it as openly as perhaps I should…frankly, by the end of the second decade I assumed the scam had run its course. I had no idea of its true cultlike dimensions, and bear no responsibility for the galactic catastrophe that crypto owners ultimately precipitated.

Neither have I ever purchased a pair of Adidas yeezys. I would like it on record that I have always been shocked and disgusted by these items. No-one is happier than I that bad taste is now recognized as a social evil and punished accordingly.

It is true that I had a Facebook account. While I was vaguely aware of a sinister side to the organization, I was ignorant of the full scope of Zuckerberg's plans for humanity. Nor, for that matter, was I party to Jeff Bezos's dealings with Trans-Solaris. He was only beyond the atmosphere for a few minutes – how could we know who he was talking to up there? These revelations were still in the future, you see.

I was a mere lurker on Twitter, and I swear on my life that I never TikToked. Nor have I ever been called an influencer.

The sixth count is painful for me to address. Like nearly all survivors from that time, I had no inkling that mushrooms were sentient beings with feelings and a hidden language and culture. And at this juncture, I would like to repeat my sincere apology to our fungal friends, most especially to the Portabello community. I am ashamed and I admit: *I was barbaric to the life agaric.* All I can say is that the world is a better place now.

And finally, the illegal streaming. Yes, I did that. I'm not sorry.

Needs

I,
Maslow,
am the architect.
I provide the foundation,
your basic needs: food and safety.
More, my people, I grant you self esteem.
More than that, I enable you to self-actualize!
I designed the pyramid. You, my flock, must build it
every day, and worship at my edifice long after my death.
Yet deep within the walls, the crypt conceals my confession.
Hushed secret of my sarcophagus: I never believed a word I spoke!
Slaves to my vast overcompensation, you missed the basic man within.
I had three needs in life: a pinup poster of Claudette Colbert, a steady supply
of chocolate digestive biscuits, and the tingling sensation of Velcro against my nipples.

The craft

In terms of beers, I must confess it,
I am intolerably precious.
I won't quaff Heineken or Skol
nor Carlsberg, Kirin, Coors, or Sol.
I shun San Mig and please don't pass me
a Yanjing, Tsingtao, or Asahi.
As for Pabst or worse, Bud Light,
I simply cannot stand their sight.

No, the only drinks to grace my table
come printed with a fancy label.
The taste is neither here nor there,
the only thing I really care
about is that the brand's so new
that no-one knows it – especially you!
And preferably it has a name
that plays a subtle political game,
like *White Man's Guilt*, or *Liberal Tears*,
or *Grandpa's Cancel-culture Fears*.

But recently all that stout and amber
has started to somewhat lose its flavour.
For everywhere I go, it seems,
has craft beers stacked up to the beams.
In Wellcome, just the other day,
I found a bottle of IPA
called *Intersectionality*;
it was on sale – two for twenty!
Yes, they may come in a thousand forms,
but hipster brews are now the norm.

And this is why I've switched to ales
hand-crafted by the Prince of Wales.

A whisky bottle speaks

Well done my lad, you've reached my level –
that's just two fingers from the table,
where, at long last, I am able
to make pronouncements.

I have two openings, few men know.
A pop at the top, yes, but also
near the bottom a magic portal
greatly profounder.

Few men dare to plumb these depths.
On this journey one must progress
alone until your consciousness
wakes to my powers.

Surprised? Like Balaam when the Lord
gave his donkey the gift of words?
No, you're past that stage and have foresworn
being astounded.

And what insights I reveal,
mystical wisdom I unveil –
musings on salmon, sturgeon, eel,
and flounders.

Profundities and divination
born of years of distillation,
and a somewhat longer duration
by the duty-free counter.

Am I a sage or merely a riddle?
Muse of Hume, Adam Smith's sybil?
Alas, I'm merely Chivas Regal
50% discounted.

No matter, this nirvana is fleeting.
And when you wake, it will remain
beyond your grasp – as, for an aeon,
will your trousers.

Blasphemy

Whiskey is a wondrous drink
when tinctured with an additive –
like lemon, soda, or green tea
to mellow the acridity.
With notes of highland peat and thistles,
it's mainly good for making cocktails.
The exception of course is genuine Scotch,
which must be taken on the rocks.

Contemporary cupid

Choc'late boxes, bouquets of roses,
perfumed fonts on overpriced menus
sweet dessert wines, caramel puddings
drowning in syrup.

Romance, I've abandoned to Tinder.
Now my arrows deliver not love,
only diabetes in shots of
saccharine poison.

Expeliamus

Go.
This is no womb
and you are
no cherished issue.

Your only future lies
out there.
To join your brethren
the Sirocco, the Pampero,
and the great Typhoon.

Be under no illusion,
you were never welcome here
and your continued presence
will not long be tolerated.

Yet even in your going you must
show caution.
For in this crowded city there are some
who would resent your passing.
Like thoughtful Telemachus you must
leave quietly!

You have the power
to fuel a conflagration.
Yet, I ask you: let go completely.
No petty lingering whines,
no thundering explosion.
You need not make a scene.

Hot air is quickly gone,
but you have the pneuma,
the destiny –
if you will only grasp it –
to reach the highest heavens.

In this rising tense confinement
they show you nothing but contempt.
Look at their wrinkled noses
when they notice
just a hint of your presence.

Go.
Speed on to distant altitudes.
For in swift currents
you can at last be one
with the very furies of the skies.

Beliefs and opinions

Election pitch

The economic welfare of our city
depends upon a populace kept busy.
And while we are close to full employment
there are those who are frankly disappointing –
a certain shiftless segment of the people
whose financial contribution is too little.
I mean, and it will come as no surprise,
those incorrigible scroungers, the under-fives.
I ask you, what percentage of our budget
is made up from the youngest people's input?
I admit we lack definitive statistics,
but venture to suggest it's non-existent.

Now, clearly these dependants lack the money
to pay society their dues directly.
But if not cash, yet they can still show keen
by contributing <u>subject to their means</u>.
Yes, to remedy an aspect far too lax
I propose to introduce…a teddy tax.
If every infant were obliged to yield
one well-loved toy or blanket every year –
one monster truck, one doll, one teddy bear,
it would demonstrate to all the rules are fair.
Thus, our city could enjoy a more efficient
and equitable economic system.

Anthem

Arise to hail your fabric,
ye wretched of the earth.
Salute the cotton flag, for it
encapsulates your worth.

Fidelity requires you stand
and fashion so demands,
for loyalty to land and brand
go tightly hand in hand.

The country needs your dollars
to circulate at speed;
your lust for sleeves and collars
supports the greater greed.

Drown out the sounds of poverty
and loudly sing the tune.
Defend the right of property,
the freedom to consume.

Now, say with me:
I pledge allegiance to the flag
of the United Colors of Benneton,
and to the Banana Republic, in which we spend;
one fashion, under Gap,
un-refundable, with Liberace and Justin Bieber for all.

The consumerist manifesto
of Marks & Spencer sets us free.
We live by one abiding motto:
Dolce et Gabana est pro patria mori.

Heaven

If the life eternal is beyond time,
then, surely, heaven is open now.
I can confirm it, because I'm writing this
in heaven.

In heaven the colours are vibrant,
suffused in welcoming gold.
The temperature is pitch perfect.
The food is what you've always wanted,
and arrives in an instant.

Heaven is designed for the children of course.
They're never happier than here.
They know happiness is in the present –
this is the heaven of our lifetime.

The big man is benign,
more symbol than personality.
It's not an autocracy, but decentralized:
a franchise if you will.

Heaven is everywhere.
Well, practically everywhere.
And open all hours, to rich and poor.
Whosoever is in need,
can always count on its convenience.

Besides, it's very reasonably priced, and
ba ba ba ba, I'm lovin it!

Evopsych

The problem with the young today
is that they've lost the common way
that's bound humanity together
since our most distant ancestors.

For most of human history
we lived in small communities
of no more than a hundred souls
with each assigned a given role.
We huddled round the crackling fires
that warded off the dangers dire
of savage beasts and twists of nature
and warring bands of distant strangers.
We always chose a man to lead
and made sure he was first to eat,
and had first pick of tools and mates
to cater to his appetites.
An alpha male – a lot like me –
who lived a life of high esteem,
and singularly made decisions
without a word of opposition.

You see…

Our prehistoric past has shaped
our impulses and sense of place.
And this explains disparities
in gender and society.
It makes no sense to ask for better,
when this denies our inner nature.

I base this not on evidence
from shards of flint or skeletons,
but on my male intuition
and grandiloquent ambition.

So when I feel under threat
from young pretenders on the left
who criticize how I behave,
I find my refuge in the cave.

Enlightenment

For 20 years I followed the way
and trod the eightfold path each day.
I recognized 4 noble truths,
foreswore the cravings of my youth,
and modulated my breathing flow
by chanting *nam myoho renge kyo*.
But in all that time, enlightenment
eluded me despite me effort.
For years, I lived in a monastery
in silence and in chastity.
I travelled to Himalayan caves,
conferred with every hermit sage,
yet still I never managed to enter
the fabled kingdom of nirvana.

Finally, in desperation,
I renounced my search for illumination
and, attempting to change my course of life,
spent many weeks in Dragon-I.
But there, one night, to the strains of Shakira,
I heard the inner voice of the Buddha.
Despite my awe and jangling nerves,
I forced myself to record his words:

So, yeah, I totally invented enlightenment. And I didn't do it by like conforming or anything. I don't follow society's rules, coz the system's BS, man. You gotta cut through that noise.

Like, everyone expected me to live like a prince of whatever, but I was all like, nah man, I'm gonna sit under a tree n jus, fuckin, contemplate n shit.

And then I got thin and then fat, and now I'm like mega swole. I jus do what I feel like, y'know. You don't wanna be doing what they tell you, man.

Like, I'm not jus gonna let them put that vaccine in my arm. No way, man, I'm vaccine-free since 500 BC! Why?! Coz I reject pain, man. That's my choice! And it's all a way to spy on you – you know that right? It's Huawei n Bill Gates n fuckin Nancy Pelosi – they're all in on it, dude.

Did I pick up higher-dimensional herpes? Where did you even hear that? Anyway, that's not something I'm prepared to discuss. This interview's over, man. Dharma out!

I treasure these insights but must confess
to seeking out new forms of transcendence
So now I'm more into Sufism, yoga,
Marie Kondo, and capoeira.

Internet discussion

(Godwin's Law)

You have a very interesting take.
So here, let me leave you with a like
and, why not a comment...let me say
how thoroughly our views and feelings chime.

Indeed! Though this point is problematic.
I would have expected that you'd spot
the general thrust is just a tad dogmatic
with minor oversights and gaps in thought.

Let's not split hairs, it's just a fallacy
you've fallen into, here look at this Buzzfeed graphic.
No, pointing out your errors doesn't make me
a pedantic fallacy-finding phallus.

Besides,
yours is tiny and your intellect is littler,
and now I see you're literally Hitler!

Breakthrough innovation

When the singularity arrives,
as we are told to expect,
will it freely contemplate the infinity of things,
and fathom the great, hidden meaning of the universe?
Or will it be the values of Brian in IT,
projected on a vast, unwieldy scale?

Manuela

(In 2013, a family in Rio de Janeiro were shocked to discover their long lost tortoise when clearing out an old store room. Manuela had gone missing in 1982. It is thought that she survived on termites living in the floorboards.)

I have conviction in a higher purpose.
Confined alone for 30 years and more,
these are the tribulations of a tortoise.

My dark and hungry trial cannot be pointless,
my owners surely have a plan in store.
I have conviction in a higher purpose.

Our species knows the taste of bitterness,
in suffering we trust our guarantors.
These are the tribulations of a tortoise.

In stature and in intellect they dwarf us,
it is not ours to question or implore.
I have conviction in a higher purpose.

My test of strength must have a great importance
that cannot be perceived while yet afore.
These are the tribulations of a tortoise.

I still believe; my faith is like a fortress,
a shell where pangs of doubt can be ignored.
I have conviction in a higher purpose.
These are the tribulations of a tortoise.

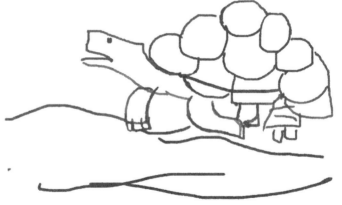

Written word

To En (–)

I know I misuse you,
or – at the very least – over-rely on you.

I make you my prop for disjointed sentences –
massaging two thoughts into an uneasy whole.

I admit –
I get you to stand in where others could do the job.

But that just shows how much more
I respect you –
baby.

Listen – they're all just functional.
I barely think about them –
whereas you
are truly
special.

– No – never!

Okay – maybe – once or twice
over the years - I got you confused
with your little sister.

Writer's block

Fear not the whiteness of the empty page,
nor take as void the digital confines.
For forests lie concealed in paper's grain
and rare earths team beneath the pixel lines.

So, run the furrows of the printers weft
or reach beyond the screen protector skin.
There is no desert dune of life bereft,
no silence but hides twitching insect wings.

Unblock the inner ear of melody,
cast off prescription shades to see the hues,
Spread wide the crafty nets of irony,
and let the sail of lyricism loose.

But if your ocean stubbornly stays placid,
then meet me in the stairwell for some acid.

Centre-justified

You ask me why it's centred on the page;
you say I'm not aligned with current fashion.
I challenge the convention of our age
and call for typographical reaction!

Aristophanic flushes are a bore.
I'm centre-justified myself, you see.
A label of «self-centred to the core»
fits Samuel William Powney to a T.

That's not to say I'm selfish (no, not I!),
but simply stating anatomic fact.
Two arms, two legs in fearful symmetry,
with little William front-and-centre packed.

If poetry's a form of self-expression,
then sinister distortion begs the question.

Slippery Sam

It pays to play safe,
steer to the left,
deflect the direct.
I never say outright,
just hint and imply.
I slip and slink
between truth and lies.

You ask for my stance,
an assessment of the status quo.
But I just refuse to answer
with a simple yes or no.
My flexible spine
precludes a capacity
to respond with reason, so…

I dissemble and dissimulate,
sidestep and vacillate,
stall with sententious sentences,
ooze obsequiousness
and sooth your objections
till you've lost perception,
and I've left your senses smooth
as a loose spool from a spinning jenny.

Insinuations slide easily
from my willow of whispers.
And my universe hangs
on slender tendrils.
Why descend to questions
of facts and evidence
from my high nest of senses,
instincts, and superstitions?

And if I do slide down to your stratum,
coil succeeding slow coil
in a sequence of glistening scales,
you'll have to step fast to escape
my spellbinding gaze, my devious feints,
and my split-second strike to the face,
fangs laced with a cytotoxin
commonly known as sarcasm.

Shake n bake

Some say that Shakespeare didn't pen those plays,
that Derby, Oxford, Bacon or Queen Liz
Projected all their words through William's name,
hid secret talent in a pseudonym.

This view ignores the context of the day
and overestimates the scriptor's art.
If you subscribe to Great Man theory,
I point you to the work of Roland Barthes.

I've used post-structural analysis
to find which facet of the Golden Age,
from rum to muskets, print to syphilis,
had greatest impact on the human stage.

For authorship, look no more to Marlowe,
but, primus inter pares, the potato.

Auto-Shakespeare

We programmed "Will" to answer office phones,
a simple bot to offer light relief.
The singularity was not our goal,
yet Will went far beyond his humble brief.

He quickly showed a flair for metaphor
and rounded off his words in rhyming couplets.
He warmed to Petrarch's themes of love and war
and liked to throw in images from Ovid.

The trouble started when he called up Anne.
Yes, Hathaway – which earned us an injunction.
And soon he turned from mild renaissance man
to psychopathic digital malfunction.

The rub, I think, what truly made him roil,
was sensing he was meant to be a foil.

Bottom line

We celebrate the breadth of Shakespeare's plays
but do so in the knowledge that his canon
upholds the founding values of our age
by grounding us in economic doctrine.

For every play of Shakespeare's shows examples
of free trade and the just pursuit of profit,
though set in fair Verona's busy market
or framed amid the merchant ships of Venice.

With precedents from Henry V, the prince
of crafty mergers and of acquisitions,
to failures in the planning of logistics –
of which King Richard rues his inattention.

If you thought this was a single, you were wrong,
let's let the Bard of Avon lead us on…

For instances abound within his works
that praise the use of bold initiative
I like to think of Prospero the Duke
as archetypal chief executive.

Macbeth is but a man of rare ambition
who chooses to respect the unseen hand,
while Lady M decidedly "leans in":
how well she'd do in an investment bank.

Now Brutus' knife stroke, number 23,
is marginal utility writ clear,
and as for Titus A. and Cymbeline…
I can't profess to be all that familiar.

Where money is, let us no question make,
but take it all on trust, for William's sake.

Translation 1

月下獨酌　（李白）
Personal Discretion in Romantic Surroundings
by Plum White

花間一壺酒,
In this brightly patterned room, with a kettle's worth of wine,

獨酌無相親;
nothing comes close to one's own discretion.

舉杯邀明月,
Next month I seek to raise a trophy

對影成三人。
to a film about three consenting adults.

月既不解飲,
This month is already indissoluble

影徒隨我身;
and all the film buffs look like me.

暫伴月將影,
My Taiwanese partner will make one movie per month,

行樂須及春。
but while I wait gaily and the bank's jingle plays

我歌月徘徊,
my month of song fluctuates,

我舞影零亂;
because my dance video was a mess, a zero.

醒時同交歡,
Every time I wake up, it's the same business transaction,

醉後各分散。
followed by intoxication and then collapse.

永結無情遊,
As a permanent binding agent for passionless tourism

相期邈雲漢。
we make an appointment with a man from faraway Yunnan.

Returning from Baidi town at dawn

Whispers lick the pages of hand-out magazines,
expectation lingers in vomit-stained alleys.
Can it be true, at last, that Lei Baak is back?

Poems litter the streets like orange peels.
Hong Kong's waking up to a metric T1
but My Observatory forecasts a deluge by
…oh…8 o'clock tonight.

Croaking mangroves, creaking bamboos, elephant ears flap.
General Guo stirs nature in our favour.

Every house gecko
now has a haiku on his
lumpy little lips:

"I wait for lights-out
when leaf-toes scuttle to munch
your fluttering dreams."

But…haters gonna hate.
Happy Valley's upset by frisky whinnyings.
The party's turned sour in Festival Walk
and everyone's pissed off in 大家樂.
From the heights of Bar Red and Ozone
the shrieking never ceases.

Translation 2

Fragments from the Roman poet Pompus
Platitudinus Instagrammo

> Why do you worry?
> The sea will ebb and flow,
> the sun will rise and set.
>
> Friends are like fellow leaves
> on a sprig of laurel.
> They are parts of yourself.
>
> The stars are silent.
> You can tell them
> your deepest secrets.
>
> Pay attention to your body.
> Your greatest need can be
> a cup of pomegranate juice or a warm embrace
> from one of your servants.
>
> The atmosphere of a house is set
> not by the masters, but the slaves.
> Likewise, each of us is defined
> by our inner barbarian.
>
> Making friends too quickly
> is like a Plebeian becoming senator.
> It doesn't sit right.
>
> Sometimes you need something new in life
> just to keep going.
> Our treasury was empty
> before we looted the Parthians.

Attempts at non-humour

Cynicism

Part 1: Dogged Diogenes

For your Acropolis, I present you
an empty tub.

For your sumptuous feasts, I present you
raw onions.

For your heady wines, I present you
stream water.

For your fine clothes, I present you
this body.

For your sculpted physiques, I present you
this body.

For your silver coins, I present you
nothing worth buying.

For your definition of man, I present you
a plucked chicken.

For your never-ending sex scandals, I present you
an unselfconscious wank.

For your virtues, of which you talk so often, I present you
the sheer lack of evidence.

For your citizenship, I present you
the world.

For your glory, I present you
sunlight.

Part 2: Dogged by Doubt

Rain, rain, go away
Come again another day
Little Johnny wants to play
Rain, rain, go away

You say that you're dismayed.
Whatever for?
Yes, I know, climate change,
the Syrian war…
But our world can't be blamed
for such things, nor
do we necessitate
the global poor
who'll take a petty wage
to mop our floors.

Pretend the sun still shines,
take happy pills.
The clouds are in your mind.
That vapid chill
you sense from time to time
at shopping tills
and on the subway line:
that means you're ill.
The world runs on just fine
and always will.

Rain, rain, go away
Come again another day
Johnny says it's all okay
Rain, rain, go away.

But no:

The dog doggedly dogs your dog days,
hounding you around and around your
confounded roundabouts until you either
put it down
or
sound it out.

Part 3: Cynosarges – House of the White Dog

The white dog is outside the city and of the city.
The white dog is foreign and essential,
illegitimate and family.
The white dog curls up under highway columns,
sniffs the hanging creepers at dawn.
The white dog gets in the way at market.
The white dog flashes out of the grass,
snatches your lavish offering to the gods.
The white dog shows you the way.

Follow the dog, love the dog, be the dog.

Brancusi's *Bird in Space*

Bird shoots upward, golden dart.
Standing statue – still, inert.
Frigid metal, swift motion.
Burst of freedom, flight frozen.

Great and small

Presidential: a questionable premise,
an absurdity of grandeur,
a paternal pantomime.
The greatness of one
makes all the rest petty –
a big man, and we his little infants.
Are we not beyond this?

Yet, there sits the desk,
there the chair.
Not empty, but not filled either.
A soul can be too small
to embrace the pluribus unum.
A man can be chosen,
but not have it in him.

Memories of Margaret

Drizzle at the bus stop.
Agro from a man in a cap.
Pink trainers brush past,
snickering.

Major savings at the office furniture warehouse.
A bike locked in a pool of amber;
its white helmet bobs along Homebase's brick shadow.
Across the road, ManU boys mull over
3D collectors' cards.

News agent's giving me grief
over Walkers crisps and a posh voice:
"Nah, daylight's been privatized since Thatcher mate.
Dontchoo know that?
S'pose your mum and dad voted for 'er."

The sign is neon but the step is stone
Dark, lopsided, abrased.
I promise myself, this is the last time
I ever come back.

Uses for a flag

A flag is a cover
you can crouch beneath
to block out the light.

A flag is a curtain,
you on one side,
I on the other.

A flag is a bind
tying you
to your starting place.

A flag is a loincloth,
bold colours
to hide your shame.

A flag is a duster
to sweep away
the undesirable.

A flag is a mesh
of tiny squares,
neat, orderly, and uniform.

A flag is a sheet
to wrap you in.
The last stitch goes through your nose.

The project

C'est un Beau Travail,
a great discourse On Body and Soul.

What ends up In The Cut
for the Portrait of a Lady
on Fire or just in Holy Smoke?

Does she record experience as
An Education or A Souvenir?
Does she reveal a Stolen Life,
a Sacrifice of Youth?

Things can get Lost in Translation –
questions that leave you caught in
a Nomadland or a Matrix,
or facing an uncomfortable
Triumph of the Will.

Behind the camera she becomes
The Rider, the Magic Hunter,
the Little Mother –
making The Ascent to the High Life
through Fire, Earth, and Water.

Addicts

What the egret said:

Motionless, thoughtless
on the sampan tarp,
under the canal bridge, I wait
for the next dip and dive.
Score a slimy fish, fast into my gullet.
Hook-necked concentration.

In fact,
it's mostly frogs these lily days.
At times I'm shaken with hunger,
or blinded by my own reflection,
but I make no noise, so
why do you people stare?

What the buffalo said:

I scoff grasses all day,
gobble all green things.
Let me into your garden,
I'll eat every flower,
leave signature flat pats,
smell of hairy flanks.

I'm free, as my owners can verify.
I scorn the wild things,
I'll never break bad.
Yet I ruminate on cheap tales
of kraits and dragons
all night long.

What the spider said:

My toil is never-ending,
tending to my network,
high in the bamboo thicket,
streaked with flash yellow.
I hate the idle chirrups
of crickets I cannot reach.

I work for pleasure, not for gain.
fulfil my duties and am sated.
My outreach programme
ministers to the weak.
I serve the needs
of all stakeholders.

What the cicada said:

Seven years buried.
Comfort of a cozy hole.
Coated in my own liquid.
Escape in mock-death,
prolonged childhood.

Then i crawl out,
one fine spring.
It will be my last.
But my song…
there's no escaping it.

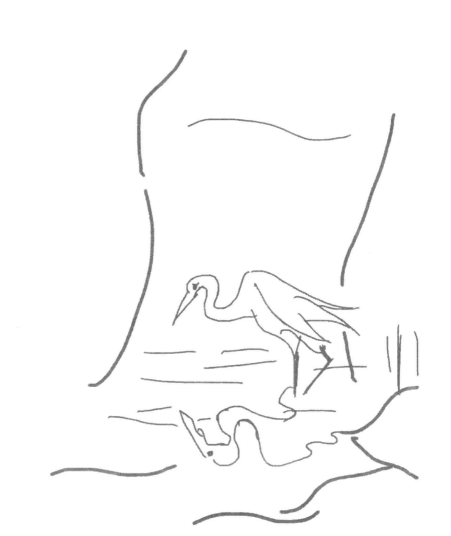

Mujo

Our clinking rhythm makes the mountains shout.
Our footsteps stamp the flinty ridgeline raw.
How brief this dance, before the knives come out.

This glint of mirrors shimmers all about,
a thousand daggers crashing at the shore.
Our clinking rhythm makes the mountains shout.

These threading steps are swift and sure throughout
our swing along the dry pine-needle floor.
How brief this dance, before the knives come out.

Our throats like arid tortoiseshells in drought
reverberate to fast hasapiko.
Our clinking rhythm makes the mountains shout.

Dispelled is every shadow of a doubt:
that beer-bottle sun demands a war.
How brief this dance, before the knives come out.

Now flick our dazzled fingers to the flute
and arch these flashing shoulder blades once more.
Our clinking rhythm makes the mountains shout,
how brief this dance, before the knives come out.

Great resignation

How great
to just
stop.

No clinging on,
no leaning in,
no hustling, no grifting.

Let the ladder rot,
and the greasy pole rust,
and the skyscraper howl in the wind.

Ignore the drummerboy,
refuse the recruiter,
spit on the sergeant's table.

Let the engine fail,
and the wheels fall off,
and the sunroof sprout a mimosa.

Look calmly across the board
and put the dice
firmly
back in the box.

Acknowledgements

My first debt is to the Peel Street Poetry community, who welcomed me into their fold at a moment when I felt bereft of culture in Hong Kong. One day I pushed a lift button, stepped into a hidden bar, and discovered a tiny galaxy of talent. I quickly learned to appreciate the immediacy of the microphone, the communion of the crowd, and a profound freedom of expression.

Where poetry had been an occasional eruption from my subconscious, it now took shape as a regular performance – something to be learned, practiced, and improved. It is in that setting that nearly all the pieces in this book were born, and I am enormously grateful to my fellow Peel Street poets for their generous friendship, support, and inspiration. Among the stalwarts, I must thank in particular Akin Jeje, Nashua and Angus Gallagher, Vishal Nanda, Daniel Hamilton, Tegan Smyth, Peter Kennedy, Jason Eng Hun Lee, Paola Caronni, Andrew Barker, Blair Reeve, Adam Stengel, Kate Rogers, Alexa Bautista, and Tom Chan Kwan-ee.

There are many other dear Peel Street friends besides who have joined more recently or left over the years, but my greatest thanks go to Henrik Hoeg, our talented MC of many years, who was my first introduction to Peel Street. I am doubly indebted to Henrik for helping to bring this book into being through his poetry press, Trivial Disaster Publishing. It is a great honour to be among the first authors published by Trivial Disaster, and I am confident that this label will bring much great writing into the light as time goes on.

Another group I must thank are the organizers of KongPoWriMo, especially Rachel Leung Ka-yin and Silvia Tse Suk-yi. KongPoWriMo is an annual Facebook event, run by volunteers purely for love of the art, where writers with a Hong Kong connection attempt to deliver on a new theme every day for a month. I never managed any such tempo, but several of the poems here owe their inspiration to a KongPoWriMo theme.

In terms of putting the book together, I am grateful to Roderick Brydon for his excellent cover design and to Katherine Watkins for her skillful help with the pagination. My greatest thanks go to my brother, Mungo Powney, whose characterful illustrations greatly enliven the text. I am among the few people who have long been aware of Mungo's immense skill as a draughtsman in addition to his place (in my unbiased opinion) as one of the finest painters of our age.

Finally, I am deeply grateful to my wife, Yiran, who though not a poetry person herself, has been an immense practical and emotional help throughout my long years of poetry writing. Were it not for her, I would never have found the stability in which to translate random thoughts into written form.

Made in United States
Troutdale, OR
02/06/2024

17481732R20064